الإهداء

إلى قلوب وأرواح احتضنتني بقلبٍ وروحٍ، وكانت معي منذ أول نبضة إلى أن استطعتُ أن أكوِّن لغة جديدة تتحدث عن إنسان بكلامٍ أو كلمات خاصة جداً إلى والديّ.

إلى أغلى ما في الوجود: أبي، وأمي.

Dedication

To those hearts that embraced me and witnessed my very first beat till I turned out to be capable of forming a new language that talks of a person with very special words:

To my parents, to my precious father and mother.

رؤى عبد الخالق
Ruaa Abdulkhaliq

كلمات خاصة جداً

VERY SPECIAL WORDS

AUSTIN MACAULEY PUBLISHERS™
LONDON • CAMBRIDGE • NEW YORK • SHARJAH

Copyright © Ruaa Abdulkhaliq 2022

The right of Ruaa Abdulkhaliq to be identified as author of this work has been asserted by the author in accordance with Federal Law No. (7) of UAE, Year 2002, Concerning Copyrights and Neighboring Rights.

All rights reserved. No part of this publication may be reproduced, stored in a retrieval system, or transmitted in any form or by any means, electronic, mechanical, photocopying, recording, or otherwise, without the prior permission of the publishers.

Any person who commits any unauthorized act in relation to this publication may be liable to legal prosecution and civil claims for damages.

The age group that matches the content of the books has been classified according to the age classification system issued by the National Media Council.

ISBN – 9789948817789 – (Paperback)
ISBN – 9789948817871 – (E-Book)

Application Number: MC-10-01-1435949
Age Classification: E

Printer Name: iPrint Global Ltd
Printer Address: Witchford, England

First Published 2022
AUSTIN MACAULEY PUBLISHERS FZE
Sharjah Publishing City
P.O Box [519201]
Sharjah, UAE
www.austinmacauley.ae
+971 655 95 202

لنرسم خطانا على أوراق الزمن، ولنزين حياتنا بألوان العمر، ولنعمل على صورنا؛ لتكوُن مِن أغلى الصور وأجملها، ولنضع إطاراً يناسبُ حياةً نملكُها، ولتكون كما نريد؛ لأنها ليست للبيع.

Let's draw our steps on the time sheets, decorate our life with the colors of age, and work on our pictures to make them the most expensive and beautiful. Let's put a frame that fits our own life, and make it as we want; since it is not for sale.

غريبة هي الدنيا بكل ما فيها، نسمع فيها أشياء لا نريد أن نسمعها، ونرى فيها أشياء تحيرنا، ونعيش فيها لحظات ومواقف لا تشبهنا، ومع كل ذلك، نحن نعيش ونستمر؛ لأننا نعرف ونؤمن أنَّ الشّمس لا تتوقف عن الشروق كل يوم.

So weird is this world that we hear things we do not want to hear, and we see things that perplex us. We experience moments and situations do not match who we really are. Nonetheless, we live and persist to exist due to our faith that the sun never stops shining every day.

من الجميل أن نعرف أننا لن نعيش بعض المشاعر والمواقف، ولكن يكفي أنها موجودة حتى وإن كانت خارج حياتنا.

It is good to be aware that we will not experience some feelings or go through certain situations, but what suffices us is that we know that they exist even if they have no place in our life.

لماذا أستمر بالحلم على الرغم أنني أعرف – نوعاً ما – أني لن أعيش بعض اللحظات التي أحلم بها؟ قد يكون لأنني أؤمن بأن المستحيل مجرد كلمة، أو لأنني أجهل المستقبل، أو لأنَّ الحاضر يبدو كزمنٍ لا بدَّ أنْ أمرَّ به.

Why do I keep dreaming even though I know that I won't go through some of the moments I dream about? It may be due to my faith that impossible is just a word, or because I have no idea of how the future will be, or because the present seems like a time that I must go through.

أحياناً نتمنى أن نعيش أحاسيس ومشاعر كالتي عشناها في الماضي، ولكن للأسف لا نستطيع؛ لأننا تغيرنا، وأحوالنا تغيرت، وكذلك نظرتنا للأمور تغيرت، لذلك فلنبحث في مستقبلنا عن أحاسيس أجمل من تلك التي كانت في الماضي.

Sometimes we wish to experience feelings and emotions like those we experienced in the past, but unfortunately we cannot because we have changed, and our circumstances have transformed as well as our perspectives with regard to things, so let us delve into our future for feelings that are more beautiful than those that were in the past.

من الجميل أنْ نترك خلفنا قلوباً: مُحِبة، رقيقة، حساسة، تنبض بالحياة، الأحلام والأمل عنوانها، والمستقبل ميعادها، والأجمل أننا لمسناها، وعرفنا أنَّ العطاء أسلوبها، وأنها ستنبض ما دامت الحياة فيها.

It is nice to leave behind us loving, gentle, sensitive, and vibrant hearts who are dream- and hope-driven, sure that the future is their due time. What is most important is that we have touched them and got to know that giving is their distinct feature and they will ever live as long as those hearts beat.

مع واقع صعب نبحث عن: السلام، والسعادة، والحياة، ونفتقد الأشخاص الطيبين والمواقف الإيجابية، كما نفتقد الابتسامة الصادقة من غير حزن يملأ الأعماق، وفي كل يوم نرجو سعادةً، فقد نكون موجوعين ضائعين، فتمر أيامنا ببطء، والفراغ فيها يملأ الصمت، كما نبحث عن معانٍ حقيقية لكل ما حولنا، ونحاول ونحاول كل يوم أن نكون كما نحب.

Within this difficult reality we quest for: peace, happiness, and life, and we miss good people and positive attitudes as much as we miss a sincere smile void of sadness that fills the depths. Every day we seek happiness. We may be in pain, and lost, so our days elapse slowly where emptiness fills silence. We are after real meanings for all what surrounds us, and we keep trying to be the ones we love to be.

لماذا نصدق في بعض الأحيان كلمة "لا أستطيع"؟ قد يكون ذلك لأننا بشر، وقدراتنا محدودة، ولكن تَجاهلنا حقيقة أننا نملك أشياء تتخطى المستحيل، كالإيمان، والأمل، أو حتى الحياة.

Why do we sometimes believe in the word "cannot"? This may be because we are human beings, with limited capabilities, but we ignore the fact that we have things that go beyond the impossible, such as faith, hope, or even life.

وكم تمتلئ النفس راحة عندما تحسُّ أنك ستلتقي أناساً يصبح العالم أجمل بوجودهم!

وأنك ستنسى حزن السنين معهم، وأنك ستشعر بقلبك ينبض، وأنك سترى ألوانَ الطَّيف معهم كل صباح، وتلتمس ضوء القمر معهم مساءً، وأنك ستتنفس شوقاً للأيام القادمة معهم، وأنَّ الأمان يكون بقربهم، وأنهم أشبه بمطر الصباح في رقته، وعند نهاية كل يوم يمضي معهم ستشعر أنك فعلاً لا تريد أكثر.

How comfortable is your soul upon feeling that you will meet people who shed beauty on your world!

With these people, you forget the sadness of the years; you feel your heart beating; you see the spectral colors every morning; you await the moonlight in the evening, you have a longing for the coming days. Safety is being around them, and they are like the morning rain in its gentleness. At the end of each day, you spend with them, you feel that you are really satisfied.

هدوء وصمت، فالدموع تملأ أيامنا وليالينا، والحزن يطبق على قلوبنا، وأعيننا دائماً تنظر إلى السّماء راجية رحمة وسلاماً للأيام القادمة، فإننا نعيش حياة ليست لنا، وبالرغم من أننا لم نعد كما كنا نريد، أصبحنا نتمنى أن ترجع بنا الأيام، وكلما مضت السَّاعات، تصبح الدقائق صعبة علينا؛ لذلك فلنخرج ونتحدى عجزاً أصابنا، ولنفعل شيئاً يجعل الثواني القادمة أفضل مما تبدو عليه، ولنمشِ بخطوات واثقة بأننا سنصبح أفضل، ولنفعل خيراً لغيرنا، عندها سنشعر أنَّ السحب السوداء تفرقت وظهرت أشعة الشّمس لتضيء قلوبنا.

Calmness and silence! Our days and nights are filled with tears, sadness controls our hearts. Our eyes always scan the sky, seeking mercy and peace for the coming days since the life we live is not ours. Although we are no longer the same persons as we wanted to be, we hope to go back in time. With the passage of each hour, minutes become difficult for us; so let's set out and challenge our helplessness. Let's do something that makes the next seconds better than they seem, and take steps forward with confidence that we will become better. Let's do something good for others then we can feel that the black clouds have dispersed and sun beams have appeared to light our hearts.

لا أعرف ماذا أكتب، فقد جفَّ حبر القلم في يدي، وتجمَّدَت أفكاري، وتوقَّفت أنفاسي، ولمْ يعُد يلهمني شيء، فقد أصبحنا ماضياً بلا حاضر، وفاعلاً بلا عمل، ولغات بلا صوت، وحياة بلا حركة، ورغم أننا ننتظر نافذة لتفتح، أو باباً لنخرج منه، إلا أن الأصوات داخلنا متضاربة، ولدينا صراع لا ينتهي، ولكن مع مرور الوقت والإصرار على التمسك بقوة مفتعلة سنتعلم أنَّ الصعب والأصعب سيمر.

I do not know what to write; ink has dried up in my hand, my torrent of thoughts froze, my breath stopped, and nothing can inspire me anymore. We have become a past without a present, actors without action, languages without a voice, and a life without vitality. Although we are waiting for a window to open, or a door to get out through, the voices inside us are conflicting, with endless struggle burning inside. However, with the passage of time and our insistence to stick to a contrived power, we will learn that the difficult and the most difficult will definitely pass.

لا أعرف المسافة التي تفصلني عنك، ولكن أعرف أني كلما أغمضت عينيَّ، أراك قربي، وأشتاق لإحساس يوماً ما كان لي وقربي، لا.. لم يملأ أحد مكانك! وأنا صدقاً لا أعرف إن كان هناك من سيكون ليحل ما كان.

I do not know the distance that separates me from you, but I know that whenever I close my eyes, I see you near me, and I miss the feeling that I used to feel when you were with me. No one has taken your place, and I honestly do not know if there will be someone or something to resolve what it was.

منذ أن رأيتك وأنت الروح التي أدخلت الألوان إلى حياتي والدفء إلى قلبي، فأنت العمر الذي لمْ أعشِه، وأنت الذي لا أستطيع أن أرى سواه، فحبي لك تخطى المنطق والحدود، ولا أتصوَّر أنني سأتوقف عن حبك حتى لو توقَّف النبض في قلبي، فقد دخلتَ حياتي، وسلبتَ قلبي، وقلبتَ كياني، وماذا بعد؟ إلى أين تأخذني؟ توقف وابتعد، ولتعش الحياة التي أريدها لك، وكن سعيداً.

Since I saw you, you were the spirit that brought colors into my life and warmth into my heart; you became the life that I have never lived, and the one I can only see. So my love to you goes beyond logic and limits, and I do not imagine that I will stop loving you even if the pulse in my heart stops. You broke into my life and stole my heart, and turned my state of being upside down, and what next? Where are you taking me? Stop and walk away. Live the life that I wish for you, and be happy.

أبحثُ عن كلمات في ضوء النهار، وعند غروب الشّمس، وفي ظلمة الليل، وأبحث في أفكاري السوداء، لا أجد شيئاً، قد يكون لأنَّ كل ما أقوم به لا يملك القيمة التي أريدها، فأبدأ بالبحث مرات إلى أن يغمرني نور الذِّكْرِ كموج البحر الهائج، فيُطفِىء نيران وحشة الطريق في نفسي لأعود من جديد لأتنفس كإنسان يُولَد من جديد.

I search for words in the light of day, at sunset, and in the darkness of the night. I also search in my deep thoughts, but I find nothing. This may be because everything I do doesn't have the value I want, so I start searching over and over until the light of God's invocation submerge me like the raging waves of the sea, extinguishing the fires and desolation of my soul, to start breathing as a reborn human being.

لو أدركنا أننا نسير في أقدار كتبت لنا، لسرنا مطمئنين بأنَّ: الأمس، واليوم، والغد مصيرٌ محسوم.

If we realize that we are heading to destinies that have been set for us, we will be assured that yesterday, today, and tomorrow are settled fates.

سبقني الزَّمن، وأخذ جزءاً من روح تلاشت في لحظة كان الوجع فيها أقوى من عالمٍ أسكن فيه.

Time preceded me and stole a part of a spirit that faded away in a moment when the pain was stronger than the world I live in.

بدأ هذا العالم بكلمة، وبعض العلاقات تبدأ بكلمة، وبعضها تنتهي بكلمة، وأنَّ كل ما بين الحياة والموت كلمات تختارنا، ونختار بعضها، وعندما نصبح ذكرى تصبح بعض تلك الكلمات خالدة في ذاكرة البعض.

This world began with a word. Some relationships begin with a word, and some end with a word as well. Everything between life and death are words that sometimes choose us, and sometimes we choose them. When we become a memory, some of those words become immortal in the minds of some of us.

بنيت جدران هذا المنزل من ألمٍ ووجعٍ، وسكنها أناس أتعبتهم جروح السنين؛ لذلك لم يسكن هذا المنزل أبداً وما زال يرقص ألماً، وفي بعض الأحيان ندماً. وكيف تعرف السعادة طريقاً لبيت لا يحلم ولا يبحث عن فرح؟ بل ينتظر ويترقب زمناً يحوّل فيه الحال إلى حياة.

The walls of this house were made of pain and sorrow, and the people who lived inside them were tired of the wounds of years. So, this house has never lived the atmospheres of tranquility and is still dancing in pain or regret sometimes. How can happiness find its way to a house that does not dream and does not look for joy? Rather it waits and waits for a time to turn that state into a real life.

مريضة أنا، والغريب أنني أعرف ولا أعرف كيف سيأتي يوم ويبحث فيه طبيبي عني ليعطيني الدواء، ولكن وقتها أجزم أنه لن يجدني؛ لأنني سأكون عندها في مكان يجهل الوصول إليه، والأغرب من هذا أنني وقتها سأكون له حياة لمْ يستطع أن يعيشها، وداء ليس له دواء، وأملاً بعيد المنال، وزمناً يتمنى الرجوع إليه.

I am sick, and it is strange that I know and do not know how the day will come for my healer to search for me, to give me medicine? But then, I am certain he will not find me because I will then be in an unknown place. The strangest thing of all of this is that he will see me as the life that he could not live, a disease that has no cure for, a distant hope, and a time to which he wishes to return.

أشعر أنني في نفق مظلم، لا أستطيع الخروج منه، فالحال مزعج، والمزاج غريب، والطريق مجهول تماماً، فأنا أعرف ما أريد، ولا أعرف كيف أسير، أسير ولكن لم أصل بعد، وإذا وصلت أبدأ من جديد في طرقٍ توجد فيها البداية والمسافة فقط، والنهاية تكون دائماً في بداية جديدة.

I feel that I am in a dark tunnel that I cannot get out of. The situation is disturbing, the mood is strange, and the journey is completely unknown. I know what I want, and I do not know how to walk. I am walking but I have not reached yet, and if I arrive, I start over on roads where I only find the beginning and a long distance. The end is always a new beginning.

أجدُ في قلبي لحناً حزيناً يجمع تعب السنين، ويعزف على أوتار قلبي كلما مرَّ بذكرى مؤلمة، فيعود بعدها قلبي ليستقر ويبدأ المنطق بعدها بنسج نهج جديد، ليكون الحزن فيه جزءاً من ماضٍ قريبٍ ليس بالضرورة لسببٍ ما، ولكن مجرد إحساس.

In my heart, I find a sad tone that collects the fatigue of years, and it plays the strings of my heart whenever it experiences a painful memory. Then my heart returns to stabilize and then logic begins to form a new approach in which sadness becomes a part of a recent past, not necessarily for a sound reason, but just a feeling.

صفحات فارغة في حياتنا نسينا أن نملأها بـ: ضحكة أو فرحة، أو لمسة حنان، وعطر من سعادة بحياة تحيي حياة، بعمل يبعث الأمل، بعمر يمضي لهدف ووقت يُقضى لتبديل حياة بأخرى.

In our lives, there are blank pages that we have forgotten to fill with: laughter or joy, a touch of gentleness, a fragrance of happiness with life that revives our life, an effort that raises hope, a life spent on purpose or time spent to change one life to another.

تأخذنا دروب الحياة إلى أماكن كنا نجهل الوصول إليها، ويغلبنا الماضي أحياناً بذكريات مريرة، وأحياناً بذكريات جميلة تذكرنا بمرارة الحاضر من شدة حلاوتها ونقائها، نعيش في زمن يأخذ ولا يعطي، يتْرك ولا يُتْرك، فتحركنا فيه مشاعرنا، وكثير من الأحيان حاجاتنا، ونصل أحياناً إلى فراغ في أرواحنا، طعمه لا يشبه أي شيء غريب جديد، ليس بطريق ولا بشاطئ، فنفقد في هذا الفراغ أحاسيسنا، وكأنه قاطع طريق في حياةٍ تأخذ منحى المجهول، فنخرج بعدها لنرى أنفسنا أشخاصاً آخرين بأهداف ودوافع أخرى، فتحملنا للمضي قدماً الى أمل، أو إلى مكانٍ ما أو إلى بابٍ آخر نحو طريق جديد.

Life paths take us to places we could have never known how to reach. The past sometimes overwhelms us with bitter memories, and sometimes with beautiful ones whose sweetness and purity remind us of the bitterness of the present time. We live in an age that takes and does not give, that leaves and cannot be left. So, we are controlled by our feelings, and often our needs, and sometimes we reach an emptiness in our souls, which doesn't taste like any new strange thing. It is neither a road nor a beach, and finally in this emptiness we lose our feelings as if we were a bandit in a life that is headed towards the unknown. Afterwards, we see ourselves as other people with other goals and motives that push us forward to hope, or to somewhere or another gate to a new realm.

حتى نكون الحلم الذي نريد لنضيء أيامنا بـ الحب، والتفاؤل؛ لنتنفس بإيجابية، وننشر السعاد، ولنبتسم؛ ولنكون فرحة في عمر الإنسانية.

To achieve the dream we desire, our days should be lit with love and optimism so let's breathe positively, spread happiness, smile, and be a source of joy in the lifetime of humanity.

نعاتبُ الزَّمن على عمرٍ يفنى، وتمضي الثواني ونحن نتساءل: هل هناك عمل يروي عطش متفائل، أو أمل يتجدد في حياة مريض، أو حق يعود لمظلوم، أو ابتسامة تبهج وجه طفل، أو وطن يحضن لاجئاً، أو حب يملأ القلوب، أو قناعة تقف في وجه الأشرار، أو خير يغلب فاسداً أو إيمان يعطي القوة لحزين، أو احترام يسود المجتمع؟

كلها أمانٍ تبدو كأحلام، ولكن عندما نكون معاً هي حقيقة، ربما نراها يوماً ما.

We blame time for an age that perishes. Seconds pass while we wonder: Is there anything that can fulfill an optimistic thirst, renewed hope in the life of a sick person, a right that belongs to an oppressed person, a smile that cheers the face of a child, a country that embraces a refugee, a love that fills hearts, a conviction that stands in the face of tyrants, the good that overcomes the corrupt, the faith that gives strength to the sad, or the respect that prevails in society?

All my wishes seem like dreams, but when we are together, they turn into a reality that we may see one day.

يملكُ كل وسامة الرجال، ودفء الشّمس في الربيع، وقلباً ينبض بحب وشجاعة، ومع كل ذلك قطعة من قلبي.

How handsome is he; a man with the warmth of the sun in the spring, with a heart beating with love and courage. Above all, he has a piece of my heart.

حلم آخر يضيع بين صفحات الزمن وأوراق الحياة، فمتى تتحقق الأحلام؟ ومتى تصفو الأرواح؟ ومتى يملأ الرضا قلوبنا؟ نخطو كل يوم خطوات من أعمارنا تأخذ منا الكثير، فنسير باتجاه المستحيل، والماضي فيه أسهل من الحاضر والمستقبل، والطموحات والأماني منسية، نعجز في هذا الزمن عن أبسط الأمور بالرغم من أنَّ الغد يحملُ الكثير باختلاف سطوره وكلماته، ويكتب قصصاً من أحاسيس ومشاعر قد تكون هي هويتنا.

Another dream is lost between the pages of time and the papers of life, so when will dreams be achieved? When will the souls be purified? When will the contentment fill our hearts? Every day we take exhausting steps through our lives, walking towards the impossible. In this impossible, the past is easier than the present and the future, ambitions and aspirations are forgotten. In this age, we are unable to achieve the simplest things despite the fact that tomorrow promises a lot with its different lines and words, and writes stories of feelings and sensations that may shape our identity.

أضواء شارع هذه الحياة مخيفة، فقد رأت الكثير: العذاب، والجوع، والألم، ورأت حيوات تنتهي، ورأت آلاماً تُدفن، وحقوقاً تضيع، وطموحات تُذبح، ورأت دموعاً تُذرف، وقلوباً تئن، ودماً يُسفك، وقهراً لا يبرد، ورأت ذلاً قائماً، وبالمقابل رأت: أحلام الشباب، وبراءة الأطفال، وحكمة الشياب، وحنان الآباء والأمهات، وعطاء البعض، ودفء البعض الآخر، ورأت خيراً باقياً لقيام الساعة، كلها مجتمعة في العالم ذاته.

The lights of life street are frightening, it witnessed a lot: torment, hunger, pain, lives that ended, pains that were buried, rights that were lost, aspirations that were slaughtered, tears, groaning hearts, blood that was shed everywhere, uneased oppression, and standing humiliation. In return, it witnessed the dreams of youth, the innocence of children, the wisdom of youth, the gentleness of fathers and mothers, the generosity of some, the warmth of others, as well as charity that will remain till the doomsday, all together in the same world.

أتعبتنا أحلامنا، فهل نتوقف عن الحلم أم ننسى؟ تبدو أحلامنا مستحيلة، ولكنها ممكنة، وعندما نسير نشعر أحياناً أنَّ شيئاً يرجعنا خطوات إلى الوراء، وبين هذا وذاك فجوة، فنقف وننتظر على حافتها فرجاً ونوراً، نؤمن تماماً أننا على طريق نسير فيه حتى وإن كان صعباً.

Our dreams exhausted us. Should we stop dreaming or forget about our dreams? Our dreams seem impossible, but in fact they are possible. When we step forward, we sometimes feel that something pulls us back, and between this and that there is a gap, we stand and wait on its edge for a relief and light, we fully believe that we are on a path that we have to take even if it is difficult.

بسبب رجل أدركت أنَّ هناك ملائكة تعيش بيننا، وتحرس هذا الكون بعينٍ تعكس الشروق، وتعطي الأمل لمجرةٍ بأكملها قد لا يكون جانبي، ولكن يحمل نبضة مني تذكره بأنه استثناء بكل المعاني.

Because of a man, I realized that there are angels living among us, guarding this universe with an eye that reflects the sunrise, and gives hope to an entire galaxy. He may not be beside me, but surely holds a pulse of me that reminds him that he is an exception in every sense.

أحياناً نظنُّ أنها النهاية، وأنَّ الحياة توقفت، وأننا أخذنا نصيبنا من السعادة، ونصيبنا من الألم، ولكن بعد فترة نتذكر أناساً عاشوا معنا، وما زالوا معنا بالرغم من كل شيء نعود بعدها وكأن السلام سكن في قلوبنا، وأنَّ الحياة أصبحت أمامنا وأفضل مما كانت عليه، وأنَّ الصِّعاب التي مررنا بها ما هي إلا واقع حدث لنعرف ما هو الأهم، وأننا لمسنا حقيقة عمر الإنسان الذي لا يمر دون أن نشعر وندرك جوانب الحياة باختلافها.

Sometimes we think that it is the end, life has stopped, and that we have taken our share of happiness, and our share of pain, but after a while we remember people who lived with us, and are still with us despite everything. After that, we feel as if peace filled our hearts, and life has become open before us and better than it was before. We recognize the difficulties which we have gone through are nothing but a reality that was achieved just to teach us what is most important, and we have grasped the reality of human life that does not pass without making us feel and realize the different aspects of it.

خيال أنتَ أم حقيقة؟ جئت من عالم أحلامي وذهبت بعد أن التقيت بك، ويبدو الآن أنَّ ذكراك قدري، وأنك لغيري قدر.

Are you a fiction or reality? You came from the world of my dreams and went away after I met you. Now, it seems that your memory is my destiny, and you are a destiny for somebody else.

لم أكن أعرف أنَّ ما فعلته سيكلفني عمراً، وأنَّ غيابك سيسلبني السلام، وأنني مهما فعلت، فلن أستطيع تغيير ما حصل، وأنَّ القادم سيكون بدونك، وأنك أصبحت ذكرى لن تتكرر، ولكن عزائي أن تكون يوماً ما حاضراً جميلاً أشهده حتى وإن لم تكن فيه بجانبي.

I did not know that what you did would cost me an entire lifetime, that your absence would rob me of peace, that whatever I did, I would not be able to change what happened, that you will not be there in my future, and that you had become a memory that would not be repeated. But my consolation is that one day you will be a beautiful present that I witness even if you are not beside me.

كنت مُخطئة، فأنا لم أتركه، هو الذي اختار أن يتركني، فاختار طريقاً لست فيه، طريقاً فيه حلم، فيه سعادة، ولكن لست فيه.

I was wrong because I did not leave him. He chose to leave me, he chose a path away from me, a path in which there is a dream and happiness, but I am not in it.

رحلتُ وأنت باقٍ في مكان خاص جداً، كشجرة تثمر أملاً يتجدد، فكل يوم تظلل أجزاء من قلبي لم يلمسها أحد كمحمية لا يمكن لأحد الوصول إليها، حيث تبقيها نقية بريئة صافية كوردة بيضاء في ربيعها الأول.

You left while remaining in a very special place, like a tree that bears endless hope. Every day it shades parts of my heart that no one has entered, as a sanctuary that no one can access, to keep it pure, innocent and pure as a white rose in its first spring.

إلى أين وصلنا؟ وإلى أين سنصل؟ أي حياة تكون بعد صمت ممزوج بألم وندم وعتاب يحمل الكثير من الحب؟ وهذا مع ذاك مكتوب مكبوت في صدورنا لا نستطيع مواجهته ولا البوح به، لذلك الحال كما هي منذ زمن والواقع أنها تغذي أفكاراً ومعتقدات لا تمت بصلة للحقيقة، والأهم أنها تطبق علينا أحياناً، فنجد صعوبة في التعايش معها، ولحظتها يجب أنْ نحل كل تلك التراكمات، وأن نؤمن أنَّ الآتي سيكون أفضل؛ لأننا إن لم نفعل، فسيكون عندها اليأس أمامنا ولا طريق غيره.

Where have we stopped? Where will we get to? What life will be after a silence mixed with pain, remorse and reproach that carries a lot of love? And this is, however, destined and repressed in our chests that we can neither confront it nor reveal it. So this is the case as it has been for a long time, and in fact it feeds ideas and beliefs that are irrelevant to the truth. The most important thing is that they sometimes attack us, so we find it difficult to coexist with it, and at that moment we must resolve all these accumulations and believe that what is to come will be better because if we do not, despair will guide us, and we will find no other way.

الحرمان تلك الكلمة التي توجع بمجرد ذكرها أياً كان نوعه وحالته ووقته "حرمان"، فهي تجرح وتؤلم القلب بسكين، وتأخذ من صاحبه جزءاً من مُلك لن يكون من حقه.

Deprivation! The word that hurts just by mentioning it, regardless of its type, condition and time, is "deprivation". It cuts and wounds the heart, and takes from its owner a portion of property that they can never have.

لماذا تبدو كل الطرق مغلقة بالرغم من أن الحياة مستمرة؟ لماذا نشعر أحياناً أننا توقفنا بالرغم من أننا نتنفس، هل هو العجز أم القدر؟ هل نملك شيئاً من الغد أم أنَّ الغد مجرد شمس تشرق كل يوم؟

Why do all paths seem closed even though life is going on? Why do we sometimes feel that we have come to our end even though we are breathing, is it helplessness or destiny? Do we have anything that belongs to tomorrow, or is tomorrow just a sun that shines every day?

لا شيء، فقط أنا واللا شيء، لا أهداف، ولا غاية، ولا أحلام، ولا وسيلة، فقط أنا ولا شيء، أبحث عن خلاصي، ولكن لا نهاية، فقط هدوء أشبه بموت مزيَّف يلغي كياني كحلقة أقف في منتصفها تطبق تدريجياً على أحاسيس لم أعد أملكها؛ لأدرك بعدها أنَّ مناجاة الرحمن تلغي كل ما سبق.

Nothing, just me and nothing, no goals, no objectives, no dreams, no means, only me and nothing, looking for my salvation, but to no avail, only a calmness like a fake death that conceals my being as a circle in the middle of which I stand and it gradually suppresses feelings that I no longer possess; then I realize that the silent supplication to Allah overcomes all of the above.

فشل الحكماء في وصف السعادة، وأبدعوا في لمس الألم بكلماتهم؛ ربما لأنَّ السعادة إحساس بين الحقيقة والخيال، والرسالة أننا عندما نشعر بالسعادة نعيش كل لحظة حتى انقضائها، ولا نملك أن نجعلها أبدية؛ لأنها جزء من الحياة.

Wise people failed to describe happiness and were creative in describing pain with their words, perhaps because happiness is a feeling that is between truth and imagination. The message is that when we feel happiness, we live every moment until its end, but we cannot make it eternal, simply because it is part of life.

بين الزحمة ووسط الضجيج نقف أحياناً كفاصل صغير نأخذ فيه حكمة الأمس، ونعيد فيه جدول اليوم، ونقف ونفكر في النهاية التي قد تكون في أي لحظة.

Between the crowds and in the midst of noise, we sometimes stop to take a small break in which we obtain yesterday's wisdom, reschedule the present time, and stop to think about the end that may come at any moment.

عقابي أنك بذاكرتي فقط.

You're only in my memory and that is my punishment.

بين الحياة والموت قرار، وبين القرار والخطوة الأولى نحن.

Between the life and death there is a decision, and we are between that decision and the first step.

الاعتذار مهم أحياناً، فقد يعني أنك مهم أو مُهتم سواء أكان عن حاضر قريب أم عن ماضٍ بعيدٍ يعيد قطعة مفقودة في نفسك، ويرمم ما بقي لك من احترام لدى الآخرين.

Sometimes an apology is important, as it may mean that you are important or interested, whether it is about present or a distant past, reviving a lost piece of yourself and restoring the remaining respect that others may have for you.

الألم لحظات يعتصرُ فيها الإنسان في طريقه إما إلى الخطأ وإما إلى الصواب.

Pain is moments when a person struggles throughout their journey, either to error or to righteousness.

"لا تتركني هكذا".. نادى قلبي وقتها: "لا تتركني وسط بحر ألم، بلا حدود وفوضى تأخذني إلى الأعماق ودوامة لا أرى فيها شيئاً يعيدني إليك وإلى الدفء الذي شعرت به قربك، فبعد كل هذا الوقت الذي مرَّ أدركت أنَّ ذكراك هي الحقيقة التي أريد أن أنساها؛ لأنك دفء بلا أمان، وأنا أنثى تستحق كليهما".

Do not leave me like this! My heart then called out: Do not leave me in the middle of that sea of pain, without limits and chaos that takes me to the depths and a whirlpool in which I see nothing that brings me back to you and to the warmth that I felt in your affinity. After all that time that has passed, I realized that your memory is the truth that I want to forget, because your warmth lacks safety, and as a female, I deserve both.

فلتذهب إلى مكان يكون فيه قُربك مني بعيداً عني، أراك ولا تراني، أطمئن فيه عليك أنك بخير، وأن الحرية والسعادة رفيقا درب مكتوبان لك، كقدر فراقنا، فاخترت طريقك فيه منذ زمن، ومضَيت وأمضَيت على تعاستي، على بؤس لم ولن أندم عليه.

So go somewhere in which your proximity is far from me, where I can see you and you do not see me, where I can reassure that you are fine, and your fate is freedom and happiness, like the fate of our separation, the path you chose long ago, after you went and decided on my misery, on sorrow that I did not and will not regret.

مضى ربيع العمر في دموعٍ، دموع كفيضان جرَفَ في طريقه كل جميل، وترك لي رقماً يمثل عمري ولا يمثلني.

The spring of my life passed with tears, tears like a flood that swept all beauty in its way, leaving me a number that represents my age and does not represent me.

أصبحنا نعيش في فراغ، ولا شيء يملأ هذا الفراغ، نسمع دقات قلوبنا وصداها، ونلمس انعزالنا، ولا نقوى على شيء، فتكسرنا أحزان هذا العالم، والدموع هي ما تملأ هذا الكسر، ولم تعد تواسينا الدموع وكأنها طوقتنا من كل الجهات؛ ولأن الأجساد التي نملكها لم تجد الطريق بعد.

We live in emptiness, and nothing fills it. We hear our heartbeats and their resonance. We are isolated, yet we are unable to do anything. So we are broken by the sorrows of this world, and our tears are what fill this break. Now tears are no longer capable of consoling us as if these sorrows have surrounded us from all sides because our bodies have not found their way yet.

اكتفيت بك كذكرى جميلة، ولا يهم كل شيء آخر.

I'm satisfied with you as a precious memory, and everything else does not matter.

لا تنتظري رجوعي، لقد غادرت عاملكِ إلى الأبد؛ لأنَّ قلبكِ رفضني بقسوة أفنت نفسي إلى مكان عرفت فيه الوحدة والألم، وبالرغم من أنني تخيلت الحياة في ربيعها بصورتكِ، ورسمتُ سنين العمر معكِ، فلن أعود؛ لأنَّني بعدكِ أصبحت رجلاً آخر.

Don't wait for me to come back; I have left your world forever; because your heart rejected me so cruelly that ended my soul to a place where I knew loneliness and pain. Although I saw the spring of life in your image, and drew the years of my life with you, I will not come back to you; because after you, I became a different man.

تتكرر الكلمات في سطور نكتبها تحكي عن حالات وضعنا أنفسنا بها، فلكل كلمة منها فصل حصل ومضى.

Words are repeated in the lines we write and tell about the situations in which we have put ourselves. And each word represents a chapter that already happened and went on.

تتوق أرواحنا إلى فسحة من جمالٍ تسكن اضطراب أفكارنا وتوابعها وعواقبها تعيدنا إلى مسار يبهج أنفسنا ويسر قلوبنا.

Our souls long for an expanse of beauty that puts out the turmoil of our thoughts and their consequences, and bring us back on a path that cheers us and pleases our hearts.

الحب لا يشبه تلك الصورة التي نرسمها لشريك العمر.

Love is not like the picture we draw for a lifetime partner.

بين نسمات الهواء البارد هذا المساء أتى طيفك بصمتٍ ليذكرني بالسلام الذي زرعته داخلي والأمان الذي شعرت به قربك، وليخبرني أنني تركت خلفي حياةً لم أعرفها، ولم أعشها، وهذا قدر أخذني إلى طريق عرفت فيه نفسي التي ما زالت تعيش المواقف والأحداث التي لم أخترها، ولكن اختارتني لتعطيني القوة والأمل، وربما فرصة لأخبرك أنَّ فراقنا كان وقتاً ومضى.

In the breezes of cold air that blew this evening, your specter silently came to remind me of the peace that you planted in me and the safety in your presence, and tell me that I left behind a life I did not know and did not live, and this destiny took me to a path in which I knew myself and I am still living situations and events that I did not choose, but they chose me to give me strength and hope, and perhaps an opportunity to tell you that our parting was an experience of the past.

أصبحت المسافة بيننا عمراً، فهل سينقضي إلى أن نلتقي أم أننا في عالمين ليس بينهما طريق؟

The distance between us has become an age, so will it pass until we meet or are we in two worlds with no path between them.

فلتعش بنبضتين في قلبٍ، بالروح ذاتها التي أعرفها، ولا تتوقف عند حزن، وإذا حصل وأحسست بوجعٍ؛ عندها تذكرني ليزول الألم مع اتحاد الروح بذكرى لا تمحى ولا تُنسى.

Live with two beats in your heart, with the same spirit that I know, the spirit that does not stop at grief. If it happens that you feel pain in it, remember me, so that the pain can disappear with the union of the soul with an indelible and unforgettable memory.

رحلتي في هذا العالم غريبة، استقبلت فيها الحزن بضحكة، والألم بإصرار، والابتسامة بخوفٍ، والحب بقسوةٍ، فيبدو أنني لم أعرف السلام، ولم أعالج كل ذلك بالتأمل، بل أخفيت كل هذه المشاعر خلفي على كاهلي، واستمريت بالبحث خارج عالمي قبل التعرف على نفسي، وأهدرت كثيراً من الدموع التي كان يجب أن تنير الظلمة التي حجبت عني الفاصل بين الواقع والخيال.

My journey in this world is strange, in which I receive sadness with laughter, receive pain with persistence, receive smile with fear, and receive love with cruelty. It seems that I did not know peace, and I did not treat all these with meditation, instead I hid all these feelings behind my shoulders, and continued to search outside my world before getting to know myself, and shed many tears that should have enlightened the darkness that obscured the line between reality and fiction for me.

نلبس وجوهاً لا نشعر بها لأسباب مختلفة، ونحن لا نشبه ما نفكر به، فنعيش يوماً وراء يوم، وهكذا تمرُّ السنون، فلم نكن كما نريد، هل هو قدر أم اختيار؟

إنها حيرة نقع فيها عند أحداث تصدمنا، فنقف فيها فترة، ونكتشف بعدها أننا أحياناً أصغر مِنْ أن نستطيع.

We wear masks that we do not feel for different reasons, and we do not resemble what we think, and that is how we live day after day, and so the years pass. We were never what we wanted. Is it destiny or choice?

It is a confusion when we fall, events shock us, and we stop for a while to discover that we are sometimes too young to be able.

أبحثُ عن لحنٍ جديد في يوم غير اعتيادي، فيه: شوق، وألم، ووحدة، وحياة، وأصبح الحزن فيها عادة مع الوقت الذي يمضي ولا يتوقف مع نبضات القلب الناقصة التي تبحث عنك، وهي مدركة أنك بعيد عنها، أجرح نفسي بكلمات تمسني، ولا تلمسني، وكأنك خيال جميل لا يعرفه أحد سواي، لذلك توقفت عن كتابة رسائل تحمل اسمك المجهول.

I am looking for a new tune on an unusual day, in which there is longing, pain, loneliness, and life; in which sadness has become a habit with the passage of time and does not stop with the deficient heartbeat that is looking for you, realizing that you are far from it. I hurt myself with words that are related to me, but do not touch me as if you were a beautiful imagination that no one knew except me, so I stopped writing letters with your anonymous name.

وضعت ذكراك على قاربٍ في بحر يمتد إلى ما لانهاية، وجعلته يبحر إلى أن تجمعنا الأيام، وترضى علينا الأقدار لنكون معاً نترقب شروق الشّمس على شاطئ السلام تماماً كلقائنا الأول.

I put your memory on a boat in a sea that extends to infinity, and made it sail until the days can unite us, and fate is pleased with us, so that we together anticipate the sunrise on the shore of peace just like our first meeting.

يبدو العالم أحياناً كابوساً لا ينتهي، تنتصر فيه شياطين البشر على الخير الذي لا يذكر، في نفوس البعض منا خير ضعيف مهزوم لا حول له ولا قوة إلا أننا مجبرون على أن نراه أملاً لنستطيع أن نعيش، ونتعايش في عالم نبحثُ فيه عما يشبهنا لنصبح ونمسي على خيرٍ لم نشهده من قبل.

Sometimes the world looks like an endless nightmare, in which the demons of human beings triumph over the good that is so little in the souls of some of us. It is a weak, defeated and powerless good; however, we are forced to see it as a hope by which we can live and coexist in a world where we look for what is similar to us, so that we can find in our day and night a good that we have never seen before.

يقولون: إنَّ السعادة تأتي من مكانٍ ما داخل نفوس البشر، ولكن أظنُّ أنَّ السعادة هي أن ترى كل مَن تحب قربك سعيداً.

They say: Happiness stems from somewhere within the human soul, but I think that happiness is to see everyone you love around you happy.

أعاتبُ نفساً تحمل قلباً تعلق به كياني، وترك نفسي تائهة في طريقٍ به كل شيء إلا أنت.

I reproach a soul that holds a heart to which my state of being is attached and decided to leave me lost in a path that combines everything except for you.

اعتدتُ ألَمَ غيابِكَ، فلا أشعر بشيءٍ سوى ألَمٍ بعدِكَ، فلمْ يعد يهمني أحد، أصبحتُ أشبَه بعلامة استفهام لا تختفي، ولا تكف عن السؤال عنك، فأين أنت؟

I am used to the pain of your absence; so, after you, I feel nothing but pain, I do not care about anyone anymore. I became like a question mark that does not disappear, and does not stop asking about you. So where are you?

من قال إننا نحلم فقط عندما ننام؟ أجمل الأحلام وأحلاها تلك التي نراها ونحن مستيقظون ومدركون أنَّ السعادة تأتي وتطرق الأبواب، وتعيش معنا فترة وتذهب، وقد نرى في أحلامنا أحلاماً أخرى تجعلنا نعيش في كل لحظة أمل إلى أن يتحقق.

Who said that we dream only when we sleep? The most beautiful and sweetest dreams are those which we see while we are awake and aware that happiness comes and knocks on the doors and lives with us for some time then goes away. In our dreams we may see other dreams that make us live every moment as a hope until it is fulfilled.

شعرت بنبضة قلبك، ولمست جزءاً من روحك، مشاعر يهرب منها قلبي خوفاً؛ ربما لأنك لا تستحقها، أو لأنها ليست بمكانها على الأقل بالنسبة لي، لذلك هي عابرة كضباب يكسو قمم الجبال في فصل الشتاء البارد جداً ويرحل.

I felt your heart beat, and touched a part of your soul, feelings from which my heart escaped in fear. Maybe because you don't deserve it, or because they aren't in the right place, at least to me, so they look like fog that appears on the mountain tops in a very cold winter and then fades away.

بحثت عنك في كل مكان، ولكن لا اسم، ولا عنوان، فجزء مني ارتاح؛ لأنك ابتعدت عن الأسى الذي داخلي، وجزء مني ما زال يبحث عنك في: وجوه الناس، وأعين المارة، وقلوب الأحباب، فلم أجد لك مثيلاً، فأنت مختلف، وما أحسست به قربك مختلف، نحن حالة عشتها بينما اخترت الرحيل عنها، وكأنني كنت بالنسبة لك سراب.

I looked for you everywhere, but no name, no address, so part of me was relieved because you have gone away from the sorrow that lies within me. However, a part of me is still looking for you in the faces of people, the eyes of passers-by, and the hearts of loved ones. I did not find a counterpart of you; you are different, and what I felt near you is also different. We are an experience that I chose to live while you chose to abandon as if I was a mirage.

تغلبنا مشاعرنا أحياناً، فنؤذي من حولنا دون أن نشعر بإهمال مقصود مردود علينا؛ لأنهم من نحب وبعد خطأ حدث دون تردد نأسف على حال فقدنا فيه نور الطريق ورسالة اليوم.

Sometimes our feelings overcome us, make us hurt those around us without any feeling, with an intended negligence that will affect us because they are those we love. And after a mistake happened without hesitation, we regret the situation in which we lost the light of the path and the message of the day.

تذكرني وابتسم على طرقات الزمن، وعندما تأتي لتحضن البحر، وعلى طاولة الأصدقاء، وعنما تقرأ كتابي، وعندما تداعب وجهك نسمة هواء باردة، والأهم من ذلك كله تذكرني عندما تعانق أشعة الشّمس قلباً كالذي تملكه.

Remember me and smile on the paths of time; when you come to hug the sea, when you sit at the table of friends, when you read my book, when your face caresses a breeze of cold air, and most important of all, remember me when the rays of the sun embrace a heart like yours.

سعيدة لأنني أحمل ذكرى بها شخص مثلك ملأ عالمي دفئاً وقلبي أملاً، أُطفئ نيران الأسى والألم، وأبدل ذكرياتي المؤلمة والحزينة بحلم جميل حتى وإن لم يتحقق.

I am happy because I hold a memory of a person like you, a person who filled my world with warmth and my heart with hope, extinguish the fires of grief and pain, who exchanged my painful and sad memories with a beautiful dream, even if it did not come true.

لا نستطيع أن نصلح قلوباً أتعبتها أزمات الزمان، ولا نقدر ردَّ أرواح أتعبها الغياب، فنعيش ونحن محاطون بالعجز، ولن نعرف السعادة، ونحن في حلقة غير مكتملة؛ ولأننا فقدنا ارتباطنا بمن حولنا، ووضعنا وسط أفكار لا قيمة لها، فبعضها غير صحيح، وبعضها غير مناسب لنا؛ لذلك يجب أن نتأكد قبل أن نضع أقدامنا على الأرض. إنَّ الوجهة التي نسير فيها تناسب قلوباً وأرواحاً وأنفساً عاشت الكثير، وأولها نحن.

We cannot heal hearts that are worn out of the crises of time, and we cannot restore souls that are tired of absence, so we live surrounded by helplessness; and we will never know happiness as long as we are still in this incomplete cycle, and because we have lost our connection with those around us, and have been placed in the midst of valueless ideas, some of which are incorrect, and some are not suitable for us. Therefore, we must make sure, before we set our feet on the ground, that the destination in which we are headed is suitable for hearts, souls and spirits that have witnessed and experienced a lot, starting by us.

الكرة الأرضية تدور ولا تتوقف، وكذلك نحن لا نتوقف ونتغير؛ لأنَّ كل ما على الأرض يتغير باستمرار، فإن بقينا على حالنا، سنصبح متخلفين عن هذا العالم.

The Earth rotates and does not stop. We also do not stop and always change, because everything on Earth is constantly changing, and if we remain the same, we will be retarded from this world.

بعد ما خرجت من عالمي ودخلت صفحة الذكريات أصبحتُ كزهرة انتهى موسم إزهارها في ربيع لا ينتهي يقيناً أنه قدر والقدر دائماً خير وإن كان ممزوجا بألم لا يحتمل.

After you got out of my world and entered the page of memories, you became like a flower whose flowering season ended in a spring that never ends. Certainly, it is fate, and fate is always good, even if it is mixed with unbearable pain.

وحينما نلتقي، سأخبرك بأنني عانيت قبلك، ولا أريد ذلك معك، وأنني أريد أنْ أترك العالم، ولا أريد ذلك معك، وأنَّ الحياة بدونك ينقصها أنت، وأنني غريبة عن حياتي بالرغم من أنها لي، وأنَّ السلام مهدد دائماً بأفكاري، وأنَّ العمر لا يعني لي شيئاً؛ لأنني لم أكتب فيه الكثير، وحينما نلتقي هل أملك الشجاعة لترى من أكون؟

And when we meet, I will tell you that I suffered before you, and I do not want this with you; I want to leave the world, and I do not want this with you; and life without you really needs you. I am a stranger to my life even though it is mine; that peace is always threatened by my thoughts; and age is not a big deal to me, because I did not care too much about it. But when we meet, will I have the courage to let you see who I am?

قليل من يستطيع أن يترجم الأحاسيس إلى أفعال تتملك المحبين، وقليل جداً من يقدِّر تلك المشاعر.

Few people can translate feelings into actions that hold lover's heart, and very few of them appreciate those feelings.

ليتنا بقينا أطفالاً نقدم على الحياة، ولا نخاف السقوط أو التعثر، ولا نلقي بالاً لأحدٍ، فنعيش في عالمنا بلا قوانين، نضحك، ولا نفكر بالأمس، ولا بالغد، ننام بسلام مؤمنين بأن القدر يتولانا، وأنه معنا، فكيف يقولون: "إن الطفل لا يعي ولا يفهم؟"... أعتقد أننا من لا يدرك معنى الحياة حتى وإن واجهتنا عقبات ومشكلات، فيجب أن نعرف أن الحكمة هي في تخطيها، والتعامل معها، والحفاظ على التوازن حتى وإن خسرنا في طريقنا أشخاصاً وأشياء، فتلك أقدار لا نملكها، فتلك هي الحياة قصة وراء قصة تحكي عن كتاب كُتِب لنا، وليس علينا قبل أن نكون، والمهم في ذلك كله الراية التي نحملها كل يوم، والتي لا تحمل فقط عنواناً أو موضوعاً، وإنما تحمل خيراً.. خيراً للمجرة بأكملها.

I wish we were children to live without any fear of falling or stumbling, paying no attention to anyone, living in our world without laws, laughing, without thinking about yesterday or tomorrow, sleeping peacefully believing that fate takes over us, and accompanies us. So how do they say that the child does not realize and does not understand? I think that we are the ones who do not understand the meaning of life even if we encounter obstacles and problems. We must realize that wisdom lies in overcoming them, dealing with them, and maintaining balance even if we lost people and things on our journey. These are fates that we cannot control, and that is life, a story behind a story that tells about our inescapable fate that has been in God's knowledge before He created us. The most important of all of this is the flag that we hold every day, which does not only bear a title or theme, but also bears good and charity for the entire galaxy.

تؤنسني كلمات تحمل بين سطورها صورتك، وعندما تعبر خيالي أضحك، وكأن النبض عاد إلى قلبي، ويغلبني الخوف بعدها؛ لأنني مدركة أنك في مكان لا شيء فيه يخصني، والآن أنا تائه ما بين هذا الواقع وذاك الحلم.

I can find sociability in words that carry your image between the lines. When you cross my imagination, I laugh, I feel as if the pulse came back to my heart, and fear prevails over me afterwards because I am aware that you are in a place where nothing belongs to me, and now I am lost between this reality and that dream.

غلبتني الحيرة.. من علمني المشي على ضوء القمر، وأن أستسلم تحت قطرات المطر، من علمني أسمع نبضات قلوب من حولي، من علمني أن أصنع من قذائف الزمن ابتسامة انتصار بعد مشوار طويل، وأن أتمسك بالحب الذي في قلبي حتى النهاية، وأن أكون خيراً لا ينتهي في حياة من حولي، وأن أتأمل وأحلم هل هي المحن أم الحب؟

I was overwhelmed with bewilderment asking about who taught me to walk in the moonlight; to surrender under the raindrops; to hear the heartbeat around me; to make a smile of victory after a long journey of lifetime obstacles; to maintain that love in my heart until the end; to be good that never ends in the life of those around me, and to contemplate and dream, is it adversity or love?

لا تسمحي لنفسك أن تشتاق له؛ لأنه وبالرغم من أننا في العالم ذاته، إلا أنه في طريق مختلف تماماً، وحتى إن تقابلنا في تقاطع طرق، فلن نرى بعضنا؛ لأنَّ ما يفصلني عنه كثير، ويثقل كاهلي.

Do not allow yourself to miss him. Although we are in the same world, he is on a completely different path, and even if we meet at crossroads, we will not see each other; because what separates both of us is too much, and it burdens me.

اكسري وحدته بعاطفة تغمر أوقاته، وأعطي عمره ألواناً لم يعرفها من قبل، كوني له كرمشة عين تحميه من غبار الحياة ومشكلاتها بعقلانية تناسبه، وعيشي معه كل يوم وكأن العالم بأكمله بين يديه حب وسلام، وهذا فقط إن كان لك ابتسامة لا تغيب.

Break his loneliness with emotion that overwhelms his times; give his life the colors he had never known before; be the blink of the eye that protects him from the dust and problems of life with the rationality that suits him; and live with him every day as if the whole world in his hands is a world of love and peace. This is only if he is an unfading smile for you.

شكراً؛ لأنك علمتني أنَّ الحياة تحمل وجوهاً غير معنونة بالخير المطلق أو الشر الخالص، وأنَّ كلاً منا يحمل الاثنين بنسب متفاوتة، فلا نعرف نسبتها وحقيقتها مهما عشنا مع بعضنا، وإنما هي مواقف إما أن تخرج أجمل ما فينا، وإما أن تظهر أسوأ ما عندنا، وما بين الخير والشر وما بين موقف وآخر نوثق تاريخنا في نفوس من نلتقي بهم، ونكوّن تلك القطرة التي أحدثت موجة أوجعت العالمين أو أحيتهم.

Thanks! You taught me that life carries faces are not entitled to absolute good or pure evil; and each of us carries both of them in varying proportions, so we do not know their percentage and their truth regardless of how much have we lived with each other. Rather, they are situations that either bring out the most beautiful in us, or show our worst shapes. Between good and evil, and between one situation and another, we document our history in the hearts of those we meet, and form drop which brought a wave that can hurt or revive the worlds.

وكبريائي يحرم عليَّ أن أحبك، بينما تعيش، ولمْ أولد في حياتك بعد.

My pride forbids me to love you, while you live, and I have not born in your life yet.

أصبحت لدي ابتسامة جديدة عندما أراك في أحلام اليقظة، وأنت قربي في مكانٍ ما في هذا العالم، بعدها أصحو ليحذرني قلبي أنني اعتدت على الاشتياق إليه ومناجاة العليم بحالي معه، وأتساءل متى تستقر نبضات قلبي إما قربك حقيقة، وإما ببعدك عن عالمي.

Recently I have a new smile when I see you in daydreams, knowing that you are near me somewhere in this world. Then I wake up cause my heart warn me that I'm used to longing for him and talking to The Omniscient about my situation with him. Then I wonder when my heartbeat stabilizes, either by actually being near you, or keeping you away from my world.

نمضي ونترك خلفنا أياماً وساعات لم نكتب فيها ما نريد من رسائل، ولم نسجل فيها أهدافاً لطالما حلمنا بها، ويمضي من الحزن ما حدد مستقبلاً، ومن الفرح ما فتح من آفاق، وما بين حزن وفرح مسيرةٌ من أعمالنا بعضها لملء فراغ، وبعضها ذات معنى، وخلف كل مسيرة نية من القلب هي التي تقرر الوجهة والمصير.

We go on and leave behind us days and hours in which we neither wrote all the messages we wanted to write, nor recorded the goals that we have always dreamed of. Some of the sorrows define the future, and some joy opens up horizons; and between sadness and joy, there is a journey of our actions, some are intended to fill gaps, and some are meaningful. Behind every journey, there is an intention from the heart that decides the destination and the destiny.

هل يعقل أن يلمسني قلبه دون أن يطرق بابي؟ لقد أصابني حبه كنجم احترق وهوى في فضاء قلبي وروحي، وتناثرت أجزاؤه في جسدي، لذلك لا أجرؤ، وأتمناه بحياتي عشق عمر وحباً أبدياً فقط، بل أرجو أن تختارنا الأقدار لنكون حياة مبهجة لبعضنا.

Is it possible that his heart touches me without knocking on my door? His love struck me as a star that burned and fall down into the space of my heart and soul, and its parts were scattered in my body, so I do not dare to wish him only as an eternal love and lifetime beloved, but I hope the destinies choose us to be a pleasant life for each other.

كل ما أعرفه أنك تجتاح مشاعري من وقت لآخر لتسرق هدوء نفسي، ويكون لدي سلام يسكن وجداني، فيحاربني عقلي؛ لأنني الوحيدة التي تتملكها هذه المشاعر، وهكذا تمضي الأيام في محاولات فاشلة لأنسى أو حتى لأتناسى، ولكن لا جدوى، بدأ القلق ينال مني، وصبري وحيرتي لا معنى لهما، وقلبي يخبرني أن أنتظر إلى أن تنكشف الغيوم وأرى الطريق من جديد.

All I know is that you sweep my feelings from time to time to steal my tranquility. When I have peace that dwells in my sentiments, my mind fights me because I am the only one possessed by these feelings, and so the days pass in failed attempts to forget or even to pretend to forget, but it is futile. Anxiety seemed to affect me. My patience and confusion seem meaningless, and my heart tells me to wait until the clouds are revealed so that I can see the light again.

أحببت وجودك قربي وبحياتي، ولكن أدركت بعدها أنك لم تكن لي ولا معي، ولست متأكدة من وجودي في قلبك أو عقلك، فلماذا ما زلت أحب صورتك؟

I loved your being near me and in my life, but I realized afterwards that you were neither mine nor with me, and I am not sure of my presence in your heart or mind. So why do I still love your picture?

في وقتٍ ما يتمكن منا الوجع، ويسرق حكمةً وحسنَ تصرُّفٍ، ويُخلِّفُ قِلَّة حيلة، وعجزاً لا نعرف له حلاً، يجعلنا نتساءل في كل يوم عن: سلام، وسكون، وأمل... فمعه أحلامنا تصبح في نطاق غريب وألوان الحياة تصبح بلونٍ واحد أبيض أو أسود، أو في الغالب بلون بينهما ليس له معنى، ووسط كل هذا يجب أن تبقى شعلة إيجابية في مكانٍ ما بداخلنا لا تتأثر بمجريات الحياة سارية كسريان الدم في عروقنا تجعلنا نستيقظ كل يوم ونحن على يقين أن القادم دائماً خير.

Sometimes we suffer from pain that steals wisdom and good behavior, and leaves behind inability, and helplessness for which we do not know a cure and makes us wonder every day about: peace, tranquility, and hope. With it our dreams become in a strange range and the colors of life are combined in one color white or black or mostly in a meaningless color between them, and in the midst of all this, a positive flame must remain somewhere inside us that is not affected by the course of life and is transmitted by the flow of blood in our veins which makes us wake up every day with hope and certainty that the next is always good.

وليس من الصعب الكتابة عن حب مصيره الضياع؛ لأنَّ الكلمات ستجمع تلك المشاعر في سطور تريح من يقرأها ومن يكتبها، وتطمس كل ما يزعج في علاقة ليس لها مكان أو زمان لا تملك سوى أحاسيسَ موجعة مزعجة تماماً كوردة في صحراء قاحلة كُتب لها أن تبقى تحتَ التراب.

It is not difficult to write about a love destined for loss; because words will combine those feelings in lines that will comfort those who read them and those who write them, and obliterate any annoying thing in a relationship that has no place or time, which has nothing but painful feelings that are as completely annoying as a rose in a barren desert was destined to remain under the soil.

عندما فقدَتْكَ ذاكرتي، فَقدتُ معها كل المشاعر التي عرفتُها معك، وكأنك سرابٌ شهدته، ولم ألمسه، وبالرغم من أنني أحسست قربك إلا أن هذا لا يكفيني؛ لأنني أستحق أنْ أُحبَّ بكلِّ الحواس، بكلِّ الطُّرق واللغات منذ النظرة الأولى وحتى الرمق الأخير.

When my memory lost you, I lost all the feelings that I had known with you, as if you were a mirage that I witnessed but couldn't touch. Although I felt your affinity, this is not enough for me, because I deserve to be loved with all senses, in all ways and languages, from the first sight until the last gasp.

يحيطني الرعب أحياناً خوفاً من أن تكونَ أنتَ سعادتي، وأنا مُجرَّدُ كائن عابر بالنسبة لك.

Sometimes I am surrounded by horror that you are my happiness, while I am just a fleeting experience for you.

وأحياناً تُكتَبُ النهايات قبل أن تبدأ، وكأن الحياة تعطي وتأخذ في الوقت ذاته، ففيها نرى الحزن والسعادة في آن واحد، ولنعترف، فقد ترينا الحياة وجهين في وقتين في الموقف ذاته، ومع الأشخاص ذاتهم، ولكن من المستحيل أن نشعر معهم بالسعادة والحزن في الوقت ذاته؛ لأنَّ كلاً منا يملك قلباً واحداً.

Sometimes the endings are destined before things begin, as if life gives and takes at the same time, as if it brings sadness and happiness at the same time. Let us admit that life may show us two faces for the same situation at two times, and with the same people, but it is impossible to feel happiness and sadness with them at the same time, because each of us has got only one heart.

وحيدة أنا بمشاعري التي تأخذني من نفسي أحياناً إلى عالم لا أحد فيه سوانا، فنعيش الحب الذي لا يعرفه سوانا، وننسج فيه لحظات تمحو أحزان عمر، وتطوي صفحات من الألم، وتنشر البهجة في روحين وقلبين كالتي نعرفها.

I am alone with my feelings which sometimes steal me from myself to a world where there is no one but us, so we live the love that only we know, and we weave moments that erase the grief of ages, fold pages of pain, and spread joy in two souls and hearts as those we know.

حملني بروحه إلى شاطئ وجدتُ فيه ذاتي، وأحسستُ فيه بنفسي، وبدأت أختبرُ فيه حواسي من جديد، وأشعر فيه بخطواتي الأولى بعد عناء الرحلة التي أخذَتْ مِنّي الكثير، فالوقت حالياً ما أحتاجه لفهم كل ما أجهل؛ لأضع نفسي على ميزان في مجرة التوازن من يبقيها على قيد الحياة، ولأحمل في يومٍ ما اسم هذه الروح إلى مكانٍ تستحق أن تذكر فيه.

He carried me with his soul to a beach where I found myself, and felt myself, and began to experience my senses again, and feel my first steps after the trouble of the journey that took so much from me, because time now is what I need to understand all what I am ignorant of to put myself on a scale in a galaxy that is kept alive only by virtue of balance, so that one day I can carry the name of this spirit to a place in which it deserves to be mentioned.

في الحب ليس كل ما تفكر فيه تحتاجه، وليس كل تحتاجه تريده فعلاً، وليس كل ما تريده لك، والأجمل أن تؤمن أن ما هو لك سعادة أبدية.

In love, you do not need everything you think of; not everything you really need may be desirable for you. And not everything you want is yours. There is nothing more beautiful than to believe that what you have is eternal happiness.

أريد أن أسمع لحناً جديداً لا أجد فيه نبضك الذي يكسرني، ويقتل نفسي ببطء مخيف؛ لأنك بعيد جداً بعد الممكن عن المستحيل.

I want to hear a new tune in which I cannot find your pulse that breaks me, and kills me in a frightening slow pace; because you are so far from me as the distance between the possible and the impossible.

وبينما أنا في طريقي أستجمع قواي؛ لأضعك خلفي، يفاجئني الفشل في كل مرة في المكان ذاته، لذلك أعود وأحضن ذكرياتك وكل ما له علاقه بك، ليمضي يومي، لأتنفس من جديد حلماً وحياة لا أملكها.

While I was on my way gathering my strength to forget you, failure surprises me every time in the same place, so I go back and embrace your memories and everything related to you, so my day can pass and I can breathe again life and dream that I do not have.

وأنا هنا قربك بمكانٍ يشبهك وتشبهه، أشعر بكياني يهتز بقوة، ويجبرني لأسرق نظرة، لأرى إن كنت أنت من سيكمل قطعة الأحجية الناقصة في رحلتي أم أنك الفكرة التي ملأت بها فراغ حياتي.

Here I am near you in a place that resembles you and you resemble it, I feel that my state of being strongly vibrating, forcing me to steal a glance, to see if it was you who would complete the missing piece of the puzzle in my journey, or you were the idea with which I filled the emptiness of my life.

ولأنَّ الحياة لا تصفو لأحد، لا تصدّق لحظات السعادة ولا لحظات الحزن فيها؛ لأنها أوقات ستمر، ويبقى حالك بعدها هو الأهم.

Because life is not completely safe and calm for all, do not believe its moments of happiness or moments of sadness because they are just times which will pass, and your state between them remains the most important.

وأرجع إليك في كل مرة بشوق الغائب عن الوطن، بحنين الطفل إلى حضن لم يعرف غيره، بتوقِ مناضلٍ إلى كرامة وحرية لا يراها إلا مناضل بولع قلب، بابتسامة حبيب، كتلك التي لم أرها.

Every time, I come back to you with the longing of an expatriate for the homeland, with the child's longing for an embrace that no one else knows, with a fighter's yearning for dignity and freedom that only a fighter with a passion for heart can see, with a smile of a lover, like the one I have not seen.

وكبريائي يرفض كل هذا، وكل ما أنا فيه، فكيف أُحِب ولم أُعشَق؟ وكيف أهتم ولم أُطَوَّق بهوى يجعل عينيَّ تدمعان فرحاً.

My pride rejects all this and all I'm suffering. How can I love and not be loved? How do I care, and not be surrounded by a passion that raises my tears of joy?

هل يعقل أنْ يعاقِبَ قلبٌ صاحبه على نظرة سرقها من زمن لا يملك فيه شيئاً إلا أنه أحبَّ حب البائس لسعادة لن يراها؟

Is it sensible that a heart punishes its holder for a look he stole long time ago when he had nothing but his love, the miser's love for a happiness he would never see?

لا يعرف الإنسان متى يفقد عقله عندما يتعلق الأمر بروح أغلى من روحه، حينها يكف الكون عن الدوران، وكأنك في مركزه تحمل على عاتقك العالم بأسره، وكأن تلك الأثقال تدفعك للجنون، وتصبح فيه مخاوفك وأحزانك عدواً يصعب التغلب عليه، عندها ينتهي أمرك، وتصبح النتيجة محسومة لتدخل بعدها في مرحلة الاستسلام لواقع فرضته على نفسك ونقطة على السطر.

وليته انتهى لتبدأ بعدها رحلة أخرى تعيش فيها إما كشخص عائد من الماضي، وإما كناجٍ بالرغم من كل شيء.

A person does not know when to lose their mind when it comes to a soul that is more precious than theirs. Then, the universe stops spinning, as if you are in its center carrying the whole world on your shoulders, as if those burdens drive you crazy, and your fears and sorrows become an undefeatable enemy that is difficult to overcome. Then you come to an end, and definitively you will then enter the stage of surrender to the reality you imposed on yourself and.

I wish it is over! Then, another journey start to live either as a person returning from the past, or as survivor despite everything.

وكأنَّ ما شعرت به ألم ووجع حاضر في لوحة الماضي والمضارع، وما زال يؤلم، فلم يغب عني، كما هو الحال في الواقع، ولكن تصالحتُ مع قَدَري، ورضيتُ بوجوده في أروقة الماضي ورؤى المستقبل.

As if what I felt is pain and sorrow that accompanies me in the past and at present, and it still hurts me. It did not go away from me, as is the case in reality, but I reconciled with my destiny, and accepted its existence in the folds of the past and visions of the future.

وإن كان عقلي سلَّم بأنك غريب بمشاعرك عني، فلماذا القلب يتوق ليطمئن عليك؟

If my mind accepts that you are a stranger from me even if by feelings, why does my heart yearn to reassure you?

لم يكن بيننا لقاء أو وعد، أو حتى وداع، فقط هي مشاعر وأحاسيس قيدت كلينا عمراً.

We did not have a date, a promise, or even a farewell, only feelings and emotions that restricted both of us for ages.

الحياة وُلِدت من المستحيل، وكذلك هي أحلامنا، والأقدار هي التي تختار إما أن تكون، وإما أن تُدفن فينا للأبد، عندها إما أن تولد فينا دوافع جديدة للحظات وأحلام أخرى، وإما أن تهدم أجزاءً منا سنفتقدها فيما بعد.

Life was born from the impossible, and so were our dreams. Destinies choose whether our dreams stand or to be buried inside us forever. At this point, they may generate new impulses for other moments and dreams, or destroy some aspects that we will lose later.

وإن زرتَ أرضي يوماً، فلا تنسَ أنْ تطرق أبواب الكرماء، وأن تلاعب الأطفال، وترسِمَ ابتسامة رضا وفرح على محياهم، وأن تكون إنساناً يعشقه تراب أرضي؛ لأنها مباركة وأنْ تزور نساء ورجالاً رأوا الكثير، ومروا بأيام لا تشبه الأيام التي نعيشها اليوم، فخذ منهم حكمة واغمرهم حباً، فكن كما أتخيل إنساناً ورجلاً محباً نبيلاً بأخلاقه لأرضٍ يسكنها هؤلاء، عندها ستشم رائحتي، وستلمسني قبل أن تراني.

If you ever visit my land, do not forget to knock on the doors of the generous; play with children; spread a smile of satisfaction and joy on their faces; try to be loved by all, even the dust of our land, which is blessed; and visit women and men who have witnessed a lot, and passed through days that are not similar to those we live in today. Take their wisdom and overwhelm them with love, so that you can be, as I imagine, a loving and noble man with noble morals for the land inhabited by these people. Only at that time you can feel my scent, and you will feel my presence before you see me.

ولك يا حبي الذي غاب قبل أن يكون وداعاً لا لقاء فيه، بكل لحظة ونظرة بكل لمسة وهمسة لن نحزن بعد اليوم، فلقاؤنا كان قدراً ووداعنا سيكون أجمل قدر؛ لأنه ترك فينا شيئاً يخص كلينا، كحبٍ لكل يوم، ودفء مع كل نبضة، وخير لا نهاية له لأرواح نحبها.

And for you my love, who faded away before it was a farewell, love without a meeting. With every moment and look with every touch and whisper, we will not mourn after today, because our meeting was fate and our farewell would be the most beautiful fate, because it left for us something that belonged to both of us, like love for every day, warmth with every heartbeat, and endless goodness for the souls we love.

بالرغم من أنَّ على رأسه جبال تهدم، غير أنه يبتسم لها فقط ليخبرها أنك العالم الذي يسعدني والأمان الذي أتوقُ إليه والحياة التي تنتظرني، فأنت أنثى عرفتُ حين رأيتها أنها بدايتي ونهايتي.

Although he carries mountains of sorrows and concerns, he smiles at her only to tell her that you are the world which makes me happy, the peace I yearn for, and the life that waits for me. You are female I knew, since the first look, that she would be my beginning and my end.

الحقيقة الوحيدة في هذا الكون هي الإنسان وما خلق له، والباقي يعد جزءاً من أرضٍ ستزولُ يوماً بما فيها إلا أعمالنا التي لا يلمسها ولا يشعر بها سوى إنسان، لذلك هي حقيقية تماماً كحقيقة الإنسان.

The only truth in this universe is the human being and what was created for him, and the rest is part of a land that will disappear one day, including our deeds that only a real human being can sense and feel, so they are completely real as the reality of human.

ومهما كنا متعلقين ومتشبثين بالحياة ستأتي يوماً اللحظة التي ستأخذنا من كلِّ ما اعتدنا عليه لنصبحَ في عالمٍ ليس ببعيد عما نعرف، ألا وهي رحمة الله التي وسِعت كل شيء.

However we are attached to life and clinging to it, one day there will be a moment will take us from all that we are accustomed to in order to be in a world that similar to what we know, which is the mercy of God that can contain everything.

والآن وبعد كل هذا الوقت لم أعد أكترث بالشر؛ لأنَّ الخير بداخلي، ولم أعد أبالي بأزمات العمر طالما أنَّ الحبَّ في قلبي، فأنا عالم بحدِّ ذاته فيه كل ما أحب، وهذا قرار.

Now, after all this time, I no longer care about evil; because good lies within me, and I no longer care about the crises of life as long as love still resides in my heart. I am a world per se in which there is everything I love, and this is a decision.

سكنتني ضحكة لا تفارق قلبي، وخطفتني من نفسي، ونقلتني بكل كياني إلى أفق جديد.

My heart was inhabited by a laughter that did not leave its place. It snatched me from myself, and moved me with all my state of being to a new horizon.

وما بين سائل الصباح وأمنيات المساء حلم ضائع بين الحقيقة والخيال، ليس بيدي، وليس بخاطري أجملُ مِن أملٍ وأحلى من حياة، يسكن بأمسي ويومي مستقبل مستحيل على قارب الممكن، يجوب بِحار العالم ومحيطاتها بحثاً عن شاطئ الأمان.

Between morning aspirations and evening wishes, a dream is lost between truth and fiction. It is not in my hand or in my mind, it is more beautiful than a hope and sweeter than a life. In my day and night there is an impossible future sailing on the boat of the possible, wandering the seas and oceans of the world in search of a shore of safety.

إنْ كنتَ لستَ بحياتي، فلماذا أنت في أحلامي؟ وإن كنت طويت الصفحة، فلماذا ما زلت بذاكرتي؟

If you are not in my life, why are you in my dreams? And if I turned the page, why are you still in my memory?

وبعد رجوعك إلى كيان أفكاري بعد غياب لساعات قليلة أشعر أنني عدتُ من جديد إلى وطن أحبه وأعشقه.

After returning to my thoughts after an absence for a few hours, I feel that I have returned again to a homeland that I love and adore.

دموع من نوع غريب عرفتها في حبي لك، وفي كل مرةٍ أختبر عذوبتها بلون مختلف، ممتعة هي الحياة وإن كانت تحملُ من الألم ما لا يُطاق، يكفيني أن تتنفس بحرية، وأن تعطي من قلب كقطعة سكر يحلي أياماً يسودها المرار.

In my love for you I Knew tears of a strange kind, and every time I experience its sweetness in a different way. Life is enjoyable, and even if it delivers unbearable pain; it is enough for me that you breathe freely, and give from your heart which is like a piece of sugar that sweetens bitter days.

هل شاهدتَّ يوماً مَن يضحك ألماً؟ إنْ شاهدتَّ أو لَمْ تُشاهِد، فاعلَم أنّه عانى مِنْ ألمِ الروح، وأن قلبه احترق مرات، وأن ضحكته انتصار على ألمٍ لَمْ ولَنْ يكسِره.

Have you ever seen someone laugh painfully? If you watched or not, know that they suffered from a pain of the soul, their heart was broken many times, and their laughter was a victory over a pain that did not and will not break them.

أريد أن تحتلَّ مشاعري، وتحوِّل الحزن والخوف بداخلي إلى سعادة ممزوجة بحب يملك كل ما أحب؛ لتحيي الأمان في أمل أضعته، لتتملكني ابتسامة لآخر نفس لأتحول إلى حياة تنبض وإن فَنِيَ فيها كل شيء.

I want you to occupy my feelings, turning the sadness and fear inside me into happiness mixed with love that assimilates everything I love; in order to revive safety in the hope I lost, to be possessed by a smile till the last breath, to move me into a life that continues to beat even if everything in it came to its end.

احذري من أن تخطف عقارب الساعة أجمل لحظات ممكن أن تكون...

Don't let the time steal the beautiful moments that might to be…

وأدركت أنه لم يتذكرني لينساني، فقد كنت وما زلت خيالاً لا يشبه الواقع، فقد مرَّ بقلبٍ معطرٍ بمشاعر أصابت قلبي وأغرقته بحبٍّ أحرقه.

I realized that he did not forget me because he originally did not think of me. I have been a fantasy that does not resemble to the reality. He passed with his fragrant heart with feelings struck my heart and drowned it with love that burned it.

وإن اعتصرت ألماً، فلن تشعر، ولن تدري، وكأن روحي تسعى إلى هلاكها، وهي مجبرة ليس عليك، وإنما على وجودك في جزءٍ بسيط من كيانها.

Even if I suffer from a fatal pain, you will not feel, and you will not know, as if my soul is seeking to destroy itself. My soul is forced, not to you, but to your presence in a simple part of its state of being.

وانتظر يا قلبي، لا تُبعده، فهذا الذي تحبه، فلا تخافي، واقتربي من عينيه، ولامسي قلبه إلى أن يدفأ، وأعطِ أيامه المقبلة حباً وحناناً، فلا تبعديه، فهذا الذي تخافينه حياة رائعة، وأحزانها سعادة، فلن يخذلك، ولن يرى سواك، ثقي، وخذي بيديه، ولا تتركيهما أبداً، سلِّمي، وامضي معه حيث تأخذك الأقدار.

Wait, my heart, do not drive him away, this is whom you love. Do not be afraid! Approach his eyes, and touch his heart until it warms, and give his coming days love and gracefulness. Do not turn him away; this which you fear is a wonderful life, whose sadness is happiness. He will not let you down, and he will see only you. Trust him! Take his hands, and never leave it. Accept it, and go with him where fate takes you.

وما أعيشه لا يُشبه أي شيء.

What I live does not look like anything.

ولَمْ يستَطِع هذا القلبُ أنْ يَألف غيركَ.

This heart could not get along with anyone but you.

ما زلت هنا لا أعرف أين، ولكن ما زلت هنا وأنت في عالمٍ بعيدٍ جداً يتخطَّى حدودي، قد تكون ذنباً اقترفته، أو أنك عذاب على مشاعر أحسست بها، أو أنك عقابٌ على ما كان، أو أنك مرضٌ سأعيش معه مع كل نفس وكل نبضة.

I am still here. I do not know where, but I am still here and you are in a long-distance world that exceeds my limits. You may be a sin that I have committed; a torment for feelings that I felt; a punishment for what happened before; a pain that I will live with in every breath and every heartbeat.

وانطلقت كطيرٍ بريءٍ بَسَطَ جناحيه لا يعرف الوجهة والطريق، فترك الأرض ليسابق الرياح، ويداعب الغيوم غير مبالٍ بعواقب الطريق، فانطلق ليلمس الحياة ويرى ما لم يره في عشه الصغير، مؤمناً أنه طالما استطاع الطيران سيكون مستعداً لمواجهة أي شيء.

I set off like an innocent bird that spread its wings and did not know the destination and the way, leaving the earth to race the winds, caressing the clouds, paying no attention to the obstacles of the route, seeking to sense the real life and see what it could not see in its small nest, believing that as long as it could fly it would be ready to face anything.

مشاعر قوية بداخلي أصبحت كجبل جليدي، أقف على قمته لا يذوب، ولا ينهدم، فلا أستطيع النزول منه ولا النزوح عنه، أحب تلك المشاعر؛ لأنَّها تخصك، أضعتُ نفسي، وفقدتُ كل شيء إلا أمل اللقاء، أو حتى الوداع، فقط فرصة أخرى؛ لتجعل ساعات المستقبل رسالة حب لكلينا.

The strong feelings inside me became like an iceberg, and I'm standing on its top that does not melt, and does not collapse. So I cannot descend from it or move away from it. I love those feelings because they are related to you. I lost myself, and lost everything except hope for a meeting, or even a farewell, just another opportunity to make the hours of the future a message of love for both of us.

وبالرغم من البعد يظل القلب ينبض بألمٍ وحسرةٍ على حب كُتِبت نهايته، قبل بدايته لأُكمل رحلة، فألمها حلو في حب مختلف من طرف واحد.

Despite the distance, the heart continues to beat with pain and sorrow for a love whose end was destined long ago before its beginning, leaving me to complete a journey in which pain is sweet and love is different; love from one side.

وأدركتُ بألمٍ لا يحتمل أنَّ الزمن محى تفاصيلي، ومشاعِرَ سكنت الروح والجسد.

With unbearable pain, I realized that time erased my details, and my feelings that inhabited my soul and body.

وأبعدته عني؛ لينساني ويعيش في عالمه بعيداً جداً عني؛ لكي لا أكون جزءاً من حزن يسكُن فيه.

I kept him away from me so he can forget me and live in his world far away; in order not to be part of the sadness in which he dwells.

وأنت فقط تعني لي شيئاً يتخطى توقعاتي.

Only you can represent and mean something that goes beyond my expectations.

وعندما التقينا أدركتُ أنَّ ما أراد قوله لم يكن مهماً، أو أنه فقد أهميته، لا يهم، فالنتيجة كانت بُعداً كسرني.

When we met, I realized that what he wanted to say was not important, or it had lost its importance. It did not matter, because the result was an abandonment that broke me.

وحين خطرت ببالي، أدركت أنك تسكن الروح.

And when you came to my mind, I realized that you are in my soul.

وخلق الوجع فينا جزءاً من كيانٍ ليس بغريب عن دنيا كل ما فيها ما له سراب!

And pain created in us as a part of an entity that is not strange from the world in which all is mirage.

لتدع قلبك ينبض بسعادة، ودع كل ذكرى مؤلمة لي، وتذكر أنَّ قلبي بداخلك، وروحي معك في مكان، لذلك عندما أشتاق إليك، لا أشتاق إلا لابتسامتك، فلتبتسم عندما تتذكرني، ولتبتسم عندما تنساني، ولتبتسم لأنك ابتسامتي.

Let your heart beat with happiness, leave every painful memory for me. Remember that my heart is inside you, and my soul is with you. So when I miss you, I only miss your smile. So smile when you remember me, and smile when you forget me, and smile because you are my smile.

وصبراً على اعتلال الروح، صبراً على حبٍّ لم يُكتَب له النجاة.

And be patient with the sorrows of the soul, be patient with love which is not destined to survive.

وعزائي أنك في مكان لا يعرف ما عشته.

My consolation is that you are in a world that does not know what I have been through.

وقد احترقت بالنار التي أشعلتها فيه.

And I burned with the fire that I lit in him.

ترهقنا متاهات الحياة بين الحزن والفرح، بين مشكلة وأخرى، وكل يوم يحمل عنواناً جديداً ومعنى مختلفاً وإحساساً لا يشبه الأمس.

نفكر، ونفكر، ولكن دون جدوى، ونصادف مخاوفنا عند منعطفات الحياة، ونواجه المشاعر التي لم نجرؤ قط على مواجهتها، ونرجع لنتساءل: هل هذه هي الحياة التي لطالما تمنيناها؟

كل يوم نبذل قوة في إقناع أنفسنا أنَّ الغد سيكون كما نرجو، ولكن نتفاجأ أنه كسابقه، فنخاف أن نخطو اتجاه ما نريد، ليس لأننا جبناء، ولكن لأننا نخشى انكساراً لا يصلحه الوقت، مع أننا نعي تماماً أنَّ الحياة لا تأتي إلينا إلا إذا بادرنا لنسرق اللحظات التي لطالما حلمنا بها.

We are exhausted by the mazes of life between sadness and joy, between one problem and another. Every day holds a new title, a different meaning, and a feeling that is unlike yesterday.

We think, and rethink, but to no avail. We encounter our fears at the junctures of life, and face emotions that we have never dared to approach. We also go back and ask: Is this the life we have always wished for?

Every day we exert strength to convince ourselves that tomorrow will be as we hope, but surprisingly it is just like yesterday, so we are afraid to step in the direction of what we want; not because we are cowards, but because we fear a breakdown that time cannot fix, although we are fully aware that life does not come to us unless we haste to steal the moments we always dreamed of.

ولقد أحببتك بقلب لا ينبض لأحد سواك.

I loved you with a heart that beats to no one but you.

وبعض العلاقات تبدأ بعد الفراق، وأخرى تنتهي بعد اللقاء.

Some relationships begin after separation, and others end after meeting.

وذاك الرجل تغير وتلك التي أحبها تغيَّرَتْ؛ أصبحا في عالمين بعيدين كل البعد عن بعضهما ويعيشان بشخصيات جديدة... إلا أن مشاعرهما أزهرت حياة لا يعرفها أحد!

That man has changed and the woman he loved changed in two separate worlds that are far apart and they live with new characters…but their feelings blossomed into a life that no one knows!